# COSMO'S OFFICIAL COCKTAIL BOOK

**105 EASY, DELICIOUS RECIPES**

# COSMO'S OFFICIAL COCKTAIL BOOK

## The Sexiest Drinks for Every Occasion

### The Editors of COSMOPOLITAN Magazine

HEARST BOOKS
A division of Sterling Publishing Co., Inc.

New York / London
**www.sterlingpublishing.com**

# Contents

# Cocktail Recipe Visual Index

*Some nights, you want to try a new cocktail but have only one type of alcohol on hand. To help you decide what to make, check out the pretty drinks in each beverage category: vodka, rum, tequila, sparkling wine, beer/wine, gin, and "other liquors." Create a concoction that speaks to you based on your liquor of choice. Cheers!*

| | | | |
|---|---|---|---|
| Blueberry Limeade  p. 24 | Cilantro Lime Soda  p. 132 | The French Cosmo  p. 43 | Key Lime Pie  p. 13 |
| The Bramble  p. 50 | Cranberry Ginger Martini  p. 66 | The Fresh Sunrise  p. 68 | Ko Tao Sunset  p. 82 |
| The Burning Mandarin  p. 106 | Espresso Martini  p. 122 | Frozen Pink Lemonade  p. 34 | Lemon-Drop Martini  p. 78 |
| Cherry Punch  p. 61 | The Firefly  p. 65 | Jolly Cocktail  p. 22 | Lemon Ice  p. 20 |
| Chocolate Martini  p. 77 | Forbidden Fruit  p. 96 | Kerasi  p. 76 | Lemon Meringue p. 26 |

Summer Sunset

p. 79

The Alama Colada

p. 48

Malibu Coconutini

p. 40

Pineapple Mojito

p. 39

Sweet Tart

p. 45

Aqua Loca

p. 70

The Passion Daiquiri

p. 88

Pumpkin Ginger Martini

p. 120

Watermelon Julep

p. 102

Berry Mojito

p. 55

Peach Mai Tai

p. 133

Rum Punch

p. 130

Watermelon Martini

p. 33

Caramel Apple Cooler

p. 22

Pear Batida

p. 37

Saba Colada

p. 98

White Ginger

p. 86

The Cuban

p. 126

Periodista

p. 110

Spiced-Apple Martini

p. 109

Strawberry Punch

p. 42

Dancing With the Devil
p. 97

Pink Margarita

p. 85

Champagne Dream
p. 49

The Sunroom Sinner

p. 60

Frostbite
p. 131

Strawberry Basil Margarita

p. 56

The Delancey

p. 87

Wave-Jito

p. 28

Honeydew Margarita

p. 64

Tequila Lime Granita Cocktail

p. 67

Frozen Bellini

p. 101

Agave Stinger

p. 112

Jalapeño Margarita
p. 134

The Tramonto
p. 103

The Ginger Man

p. 128

Cactus Pear Margarita
p. 118

Mixed Berry Collins

p. 129

The World's Greatest Margarita

p. 29

Green With Envy

p. 15

| | | GIN | |
|---|---|---|---|
| Jalisco Flower Sangria  p. 71 | Very Cherry Martini  p. 18 | Citrus Martini  p. 36 | Toasted Almond Brittle (Baileys)  p. 21 |
| The Poinsettia p. 83 | BEER/WINE Stout Float p. 125 | Orange Sage  p. 63 | Naughty Girl Scout (Kahlúa)  p. 100 |
| Sea Spray Kiss  p. 95 | Sweet Red Kiss p. 84 | The Pink Pussycat  p. 107 | Coffee Frappe (Ouzo)  p. 119 |
| Solerno Bellini p. 91 | Bartlett Pear Sangria p. 25 | OTHER LIQUORS Principessa (Amaretto)  p. 51 | Sake Julep (Sake)  p. 108 |
| Twinkle Toes  p. 90 | Rosy Sangria  p. 107 | Apple Crisp (Applejack) p. 14 | The Tiger Paw (Southern Comfort)  p. 136 |

# CHAPTER 1

# Ready for Some Fun?

**Good! Because these drinks** are perfect to serve when you're having the girls over or if you want something tasty to sip on while you're getting ready to hit the town. When you kick things off with cocktails like these, you *know* it's gonna be a good, good night.

# Key Lime Pie

. . . . . . . . . . . . . . . . . . .

*2 oz. vanilla vodka*
*1 oz. Malibu rum*
*Splash of fresh lime juice*
*Splash of cream*
*Garnish: coconut slice*

Combine all ingredients in a shaker, and add ice. Shake, then strain into a chilled stemmed glass. Garnish with slice of coconut.

—**Arthur Greenan,**
**One Sixtyblue, Chicago**

**COSMO TIP** Rim the lip of the glass with graham-cracker crumbs to make this drink even tastier.

# Apple Crisp

4 oz. applejack
4 oz. fresh lemon juice
1 oz. Cointreau or triple sec
Garnish: halved crab apple

Fill a cocktail shaker with
ice. Add the ingredients,
shake vigorously, and pour
into a tall glass with ice.
Spear the halved crab
apple, and add as garnish.

—*Laurence Kretchmer,*
*Bar Americain, New York City*

**COSMO TIP** At the begin-
ning of the evening, show
everyone how to mix their
own cocktail. After all, you
don't want to spend all
night playing bartender.

# Green With Envy

. . . . . . . . . . . . . . . .

1 oz. Midori Melon Liqueur
1¼ oz. simple syrup (dissolve one part sugar in one part boiling water; let cool)
1¼ oz. sour mix
2 oz. champagne
Garnish: cherry

Shake all ingredients together in a shaker with ice. Strain into a chilled champagne flute, and garnish with cherry.

**—Café Adelaide, New Orleans**

**CONVO STARTER** While serving up this drink, make everyone confess the one person in their life they've totally envied at some point.

**COSMO TIP** Try making this easy appetizer: Spoon some hummus into a decorative serving bowl. Sprinkle chopped chives and paprika on top, and serve with crudités. Delicious!

# Pomegranate-Graperuit Caipiroska

*1 slice pink grapefruit*
*2 lime wedges*
*1 tsp. sugar*
*½ oz. pomegranate juice*
*1½ oz. vodka*

In the bottom of a glass, muddle the grapefruit, lime wedges, and sugar. Add juice, vodka, and ice. Stir well, and serve.

**—Alma de Cuba, Philadelphia**

# Pumpkin Martini

*½ oz. cream liqueur*
*2 oz. Absolut Vanilia*
*1 oz. canned pumpkin puree*
*1 tsp. whipped cream*
*Garnish: cinnamon stick*

Shake together cream liqueur, vodka, and ice. Add pumpkin puree, and shake again. Strain into a glass. Top with whipped cream, and garnish with cinnamon stick.

**—Clink at The Liberty Hotel, Boston**

**CONVO STARTER** Ask each friend who's enjoying this drink what her boyfriend's or husband's pet name is for her. If someone's is Pumpkin, she has to make the next round!

Cosmo's Official Cocktail Book

# Snow Cosmo

3 oz. Smirnoff Citrus Twist

2 oz. Cointreau or Patrón Citrónge

1 oz. white cranberry juice

Squeeze of lime

Garnish: skewered cranberries

Add all ingredients in a cocktail shaker with ice, and shake. Then strain into a stemmed glass, and garnish with skewered cranberries.

—*Jessamyn Gangi,*
*Sonsie, Boston*

**COSMO TIP** Roll the limes on a table to break the fruit's fibrous cells. This will make it easier to squeeze the juice from them.

PARTY FAVORITE!

# Very Cherry Martini

· · · · · · · · · · · · · · · · ·

1½ oz. Martini and Rossi Rosso vermouth, chilled
1 oz. cherry juice
4 oz. Martini and Rossi Prosecco
Garnish: a few fresh cherries

Combine vermouth, cherry juice, and ice in a shaker.
Shake, then strain into a chilled glass. Top with
prosecco, and garnish with fresh cherries.

—Michael Wurster, St. Giles Hotel–The Court, New York City

## COSMO TIPS

Keep these ideas in mind the next time you play hostess:

● **You don't have to deep-clean your pad before a get-together** (wait to do the real scouring afterward!), but you should do your best to stash clutter. Use decorative tins, baskets, and hampers to hide your messes.

● **Make a playlist rather than putting your iPod on random.** Stick to upbeat music to set the tone.

● **Don't force designated drivers and nondrinkers to drink water all night.** Instead, offer them a simple, chic sip—like club soda with a splash of fruit juice, garnished with fresh slices of lime, lemon, or orange.

# Lemon Ice

2 oz. vanilla vodka
1 oz. vanilla schnapps
1 oz. apple juice
4 oz. lemonade
*Garnish: sugared lemon slice*

Put all ingredients in a blender with a cup of ice, and blend until completely smooth and there are no chunks. Pour into a glass, and garnish with slice of sugared lemon.

**—Steven Kowalczuk,
Room and Trois, Atlanta**

**CONVO STARTER** This one tastes like that lemon-flavored Italian ice you probably loved as a kid. Ask your guests to reveal their favorite childhood memory—you may discover a new side to everyone.

# Toasted Almond Brittle

1 oz. Baileys With a Hint of Crème Caramel

½ oz. hazelnut liqueur

½ oz. vanilla liqueur

1 oz. half-and-half

Honey

Crushed almonds

Put all liquids into a shaker with ice, and shake. Dip the rim of a glass into honey, then coat with the crushed almonds. Pour the shaker's contents into the glass.

—Kim Haasarud, founder of Liquid Architecture

# Blood Orange Bonanza

3 oz. X-Rated Fusion Liqueur

1 oz. light rum

½ oz. grenadine

Garnish: blood orange slice

Blend all liquid ingredients with a handful of ice in a blender for 20 seconds or until completely smooth. Garnish with slice of blood orange.

—Mattison Park, Asbury Park, New Jersey

**CONVO STARTER** Bond with your girls by describing your dream houses. It'll be fun to see who prefers a modern penthouse, a garden cottage, or a stately mansion.

# Caramel Apple Cooler

*1 oz. Ron Zacapa rum*
*½ oz. apple schnapps*
*½ oz. caramel syrup*
*Splash of sparkling apple cider*

Shake rum, schnapps, and syrup with ice. Strain into a chilled glass, and top with apple cider.

**—Parts and Labor Bar, Dallas**

**COSMO TIP** Make this yummy drink look extra enticing by drizzling a little bit of the caramel syrup in a swirly pattern inside the glass before you strain the liquor into it.

# Jolly Cocktail

*1 oz. coconut vodka*
*1 oz. white cacao liqueur*
*1 oz. half-and-half*
*Splash of crème de menthe*
*Garnish: coconut flakes and red sprinkles*

Mix vodka, white cacao liqueur, and half-and-half in a shaker with ice. Add a splash of crème de menthe. Shake, and strain into a martini glass. Top with coconut flakes and red sprinkles. **—Boston Public, Boston**

# Rediscovered Cherry Cosmo

. . . . . . . . . . . .

*2 oz. Smirnoff Black Cherry*
*1 oz. white cranberry juice*
*¾ oz. Cointreau*
*Splash of fresh lime juice*
*Garnish: fresh or dried cherries*

Combine all ingredients in a shaker, and add ice. Shake, and strain into a glass. Garnish with fresh or dried cherries.

**—Judson Sherman-Rose,
STK, New York City**

**CONVO STARTER** Tell your friends that this drink inspired you to ask them to reveal the sweetest thing a guy's licked off their body.

23

# Blueberry Limeade

*3 oz. blueberry puree*
*5 blueberries*
*3 oz. lime juice*
*2 oz. simple syrup (dissolve one part sugar in one part boiling water; let cool)*
*2 oz. vodka*
*1 cup ice*
*Garnish: lime peel*

Put all ingredients in blender; blend until smooth. Add ice, and blend again until smooth. Pour into a tall glass, and garnish with lime peel.

**—Fred Dexheimer,**
**BLT Fish Shack, New York City**

**CONVO STARTER** Get your friends to admit the most forbidden crush they've had—like on a cute professor or a way older man.

# Bartlett Pear Sangria

2 diced Bartlett pears
10 lemon slices
1 bottle of pinot grigio

1 cup triple sec
1 cup brandy
Ginger ale

Combine all ingredients in a large bowl. Let it sit for at least four hours. When serving, ladle the sangria into an ice-filled glass, and top with ginger ale. Garnish each glass with a sprig of mint or rosemary.

—*Fiamma Trattoria, The James Hotel, Scottsdale, Arizona*

**COSMO TIP** Arrange a quick antipasto platter to go with whatever drinks you serve. Pick up some cheeses, olives, salami, and prosciutto from the grocery store or an Italian deli.

PARTY FAVORITE!

# Lemon Meringue

½ oz. lemon juice
½ oz. simple syrup (dis-
solve one part sugar in one
part boiling water; let cool)
1 egg white

½ oz. Cointreau
1½ oz. Absolut Citron
Sugar
Garnish: lemon slice

Shake all ingredients except sugar in a shaker. Rim
a martini glass with sugar, then strain in the mixture.
Garnish with slice of lemon.

—Monika Chang, The Inn LW12, New York City

## COSMO TIP

It's a no-brainer that drinking, like any other pleasurable pursuit, is best done in moderation. But cutting yourself off after one or two drinks, especially when you're at a party, may be a little unrealistic. So use these tricks to keep from getting trashed:

● Pacing is key, so try to linger over each drink.

● Start the night with a glass or two of sparkling water and you'll have less time to toss back the hard stuff.

● Use spacers—alternate every cocktail you have with a glass of $H_2O$.

● Drinking water can also lessen your chance of waking up with a hangover the next morning.

# Wave-Jito

6 fresh mint leaves,
plus more for
garnish

Several lime wedges

½ oz. granulated
sugar

½ oz. cardamom
syrup (see how-to
below)

2 oz. Bacardi Limón

Splash each of
Sierra Mist and
sour mix

Combine first four
ingredients in a
pint glass, and
muddle. Shake with
rum, Sierra Mist,
sour mix, and ice.
Garnish with remain-
ing mint leaves.

—*Kristine Subido,
Wave Restaurant and
Bar, Chicago*

**COSMO TIP** To make cardamom syrup, boil ½ cup water, then add ½
cup sugar, and stir until it dissolves. Stir in ¼ cup cardamom seeds.
Let sit for 5 to 10 minutes, then strain liquid to remove the seeds.

# The World's Greatest Margarita

. . . . . . . . . . . . . . . . .

2 oz. white tequila
¾ oz. Cointreau
½ oz. Grand Marnier
1¼ oz. freshly squeezed lime juice
2 lime slices

Combine all liquids in a shaker
with ice, and shake vigorously.
Rim a glass with one slice
of lime and salt. Add fresh ice
to glass, and strain mixture
over it. Garnish with remaining
slice of lime.

**—El Mirador Restaurant,
San Antonio, Texas**

## DID YOU KNOW?

● For the smoothest taste, use
100% agave tequila derived from the
agave plant.
● If you want your drink to be less
tart, sweeten with agave nectar
(found at natural-foods stores) to
your liking. It's a better complement
to the flavor of tequila than sugar is.
● If you don't have fresh lime on
hand, use Stirrings Clarified Key
Lime Juice (bevmo.com).

COSMO QUIZ

# Do You Know How to Have a Good Time?

**1.** During your roommate's bachelorette celebration at a male strip club, you can be found:

**a)** Tucking dollar bills into the guys' banana hammocks.

**b)** Sipping a martini and chatting with the other bridesmaids.

**c)** Checking your BlackBerry in the lobby and wishing you were in bed.

**2.** A cute guy you just met at bar invites you to an afterparty. Do you accept?

**a)** Um, has Britney Spears been known to go commando?

**b)** Nah—you don't know him well enough. But you do give him your number.

**c)** No way. That's so sketchy!

**3.** If you overheard your new man describing you to his buddy, he'd probably say:

**a)** "She definitely loves to party."

**b)** "She's great—she gets along with everyone."

**c)** "She's a calming force in my life."

### MOSTLY As Hell-Raiser
Woo-hoo! No one could accuse you of being boring. But you lack impulse control, so your antics could embarrass you (hello, Internet pics of you tipping the strippers). You don't have to stifle your zest for life, but next time you want to let loose, stop to consider the consequences. You'll feel more balanced.

### MOSTLY Bs Fun-Loving Femme
You live to the max yet know when to step on the brakes. The reason you jibe well with everybody? You are relaxed and don't take yourself too seriously. Plus, you've had so many adventures, you likely have interesting stories to share. Now *that* makes you a blast to be around.

### MOSTLY Cs Party Pooper
While it's great that you don't dive into risky situations, you need to indulge a bit. To up your fun factor, say yes to experiences you'd normally turn down, as long as they aren't unsafe. C'mon, at least let yourself feast your eyes on the hard bodies inside a strip club—no one's saying you have to touch them!

# CHAPTER 2

# Get Your Flirt On!

# Watermelon Martini

. . . . . . . . . . . .

*3 oz. Ketel One Citroen*
*1 oz. DeKuyper Watermelon Pucker*
*½ oz. Cointreau or triple sec*
*Splash of lemonade*
*Splash of 7UP*
*Garnish: watermelon slice*

Mix together all ingredients over ice, shake, and strain into a chilled martini glass. Garnish with slice of watermelon.

—*James and Jane Nelson,*
*The Independent, Minneapolis*

**DID YOU KNOW?**

# Frozen Pink Lemonade

. . . . . . . . . . . . . . . . .

*1½ oz. Stoli Citros*
*1 Tbsp. sugar*
*Juice of half a lemon*
*Splash of grenadine*
*Garnish: lemon slice*
*or a flower*

Blend all ingredients
with ice, then garnish
with slice of lemon or
a pretty, edible flower,
like apple blossom,
gardenia, or hollyhock.

**—Celeste Fierro,**
**One Little West 12th,**
**New York City**

**COSMO TIP**

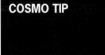

# Mangorita

½ cup mango sorbet
1 oz. Absolut Mango
1 oz. tequila
1 Tbsp. freshly squeezed lime juice
Garnish: lime slice

Blend the sorbet with the vodka,
tequila, and lime juice for 30
seconds. Pour the mixture into
a margarita glass, and garnish
with slice of lime.

**—Jacob Andres, SolToro Grill at
Mohegan Sun, Uncasville, Connecticut**

**HOOK-HIM HINT**

# Citrus Martini

. . . . . . . . . . . . . . . . . . . . . . . .

1½ oz. Bombay Sapphire Gin
¾ oz. Cointreau
1 tsp. orange marmalade
½ oz. lemon juice

¼ oz. honey
1 egg white
Garnish: orange peel

Put everything into a shaker, add ice, and shake well.
Strain into a glass, and garnish with orange peel.

**—First Food & Bar at The Palazzo, Las Vegas**

**COSMO TIP**

# Pear Batida

. . . . . . . . . . .

1 oz. white rum

1 oz. pureed pear

1 oz. lemon juice

1 oz. champagne

½ oz. simple syrup
(dissolve one part
sugar in one part boiling
water; let cool)

½ oz. dark rum

Shake everything but the
champagne and dark rum
with ice. Pour champagne
into a glass, then add pear
mixture and dark rum.

**—Rain Lampariello,
Chinatown Brasserie, New York City**

**HOOK-HIM HINT**

# Poolside Passion

4 lemon wedges
2 strawberries
1 oz. simple syrup
(dissolve one part
sugar in one part boil-
ing water; let cool)

1½ oz. Grey
Goose vodka
Splash of
cranberry juice
Garnish: flower

**COSMO TIP**

Muddle lemon wedges, strawberries,
and simple syrup in a shaker. Add vodka,
splash of cranberry juice, and ice, and
shake 20 times. Strain into a chilled
martini glass, and garnish with flower.

*—JW Marriott at L.A. Live, Los Angeles*

# Remember Last Summer

1½ oz. Absolut Vanilia
1½ oz. strawberry
liqueur
1 oz. pineapple juice

½ oz. coconut cream
Garnish: shredded
coconut

Mix all ingredients except shredded coconut in
a shaker with ice, and shake well. Strain into a
glass. Garnish with coconut.

*—Paulina Szafranski, Monarck, Denver*

**CONVO STARTER**

# Pineapple Mojito

6 chunks of canned or fresh pineapple

8 mint leaves

½ oz. simple syrup (dissolve one part sugar in one part boiling water; let cool)

Juice of 1 lime, plus a few lime slices

2 oz. Bacardi Limón

Splash of soda

Garnish: pineapple wedge

Muddle all ingredients but rum in a glass. Add ice, rum, and splash of soda. Stir well. Garnish with wedge of pineapple. —*Patric Yumul, Seablue, Atlantic City*

**COSMO TIP**

PARTY FAVORITE!

Cosmo's Official Cocktail Book

# Malibu Coconutini

1 oz. Malibu rum
1 oz. Irish cream
1 oz. chocolate liqueur
Garnish: chocolate lollipop

Put all ingredients in a shaker, add ice, and shake.
Drizzle chocolate syrup on the inside of a glass,
then pour in the beverage, and garnish with lollipop.

– Bob Perry, Smoky's Club, Madison, Wisconsin

**CONVO STARTER**

# Strawberry Punch

. . . . . . . . . . . .

*3 fresh strawberries, plus 1 for garnish*

*3 slices canned pineapple*

*½ oz. pineapple syrup (from the can)*

*¼ oz. lime juice*

*¼ oz. simple syrup (dissolve one part sugar in one part boiling water; let cool)*

*2 oz. white rum*

Muddle fruit in a shaker. Add ice and other ingredients; shake. Pour into a glass, and garnish with strawberry.

**—Fonda Tsironis,
Park Blue, New York City**

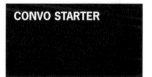

**CONVO STARTER**

# The French Cosmo

. . . . . . . . . . . . .

3 oz. pineapple juice
1½ oz. vodka
½ oz. cassis
Garnish: pineapple
slice or leaf

Shake all ingredients
with ice, and strain
into a chilled martini
glass. Garnish with
slice of pineapple, or
float a leaf from the
fruit in the drink.

**—Joe Reiser,
Woo Lae Oak,
Los Angeles**

**CONVO STARTER**

43

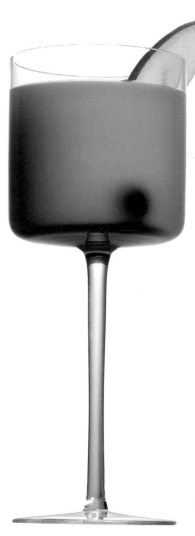

# Mango Lassi

· · · · · · · · ·

*1 big scoop of ice*
*1 oz. vanilla vodka*
*1 oz. Amaretto*
*2 oz. mango juice*
*Garnish: mango wedge and*
*maraschino cherry*

Chill a stemmed glass.
Combine ice, vodka,
Amaretto, and mango
juice in a mixing glass.
Shake, and strain into the
stemmed glass. Garnish
with a wedge of mango and
a maraschino cherry.

**—Joel Finsel,**
**Astral Plane, Philadelphia**

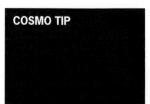

**COSMO TIP**

# Sweet Tart
. . . . . . . . . . . . .

2 oz. Hangar One Citron

1 oz. limoncello

1 oz. simple syrup
(dissolve one part
sugar in one part boiling
water; let cool)

8 raspberries

4 mint leaves

1 oz. lemon juice

1 cup ice

Garnish: mint and
raspberries

Blend everything until smooth, then add garnish.

**—Dave Greekwood, Summer Winter,
Burlington, Massachusetts**

**DID YOU KNOW?**

# Naughty Schoolgirl
. . . . . . . . . . . . . . . . . . . . . . .

2½ oz. raspberry
vodka

½ oz. simple syrup
(dissolve one part
sugar in one part boil-
ing water; let cool)

Splash of sour mix

Sugar

Club soda

Garnish: lollipop

Fill a shaker with ice. Add vodka, simple
syrup, and sour mix. Shake. Wet the rim
of a martini glass, and dip it in sugar.
Pour contents of the shaker into glass.
Top with club soda, and add lollipop.

**—One Sunset, West Hollywood**

45

PARTY FAVORITE!

# Berri Breeze

. . . . . . . . . . . . . . . . . .

1½ oz. Absolut Berri Açaí
2 oz. grapefruit juice
2 oz. pomegranate juice
Garnish: grapefruit slice

Fill a tall glass with ice. Pour all ingredients into the glass, stir, and garnish with slice of grapefruit.

**—Mixologists Chris Patino and Jamie Gordon**

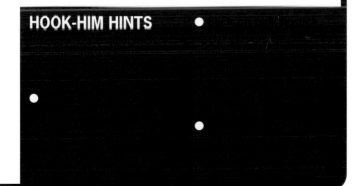

## HOOK-HIM HINTS

# The Alama Colada

· · · · · · · · · · · · ·

1 oz. passion-fruit juice

1 cup canned cream of coconut

1 oz. Bacardi Superior

1 oz. Myers's Rum

Garnish: shaved coconut

Blend juice, cream, and Bacardi with a cup of ice. Top with Myers's and garnish.

*—Douglas Rodriguez,*
*Alma de Cuba,*
*Philadelphia*

**COSMO TIP**

# Champagne Dream

. . . . . . . . . . . .

1 oz. pomegranate liqueur
1 oz. Cointreau
1 oz. fresh orange juice
3 oz. champagne or sparkling wine
Garnish: orange zest

Shake the first three ingredients with ice. Gently stir in the champagne. Strain into a flute, and add garnish.

—**Dale DeGroff,**
**author of The Craft of the Cocktail**

**DID YOU KNOW?**

# The Bramble

. . . . . . . . . . . . . .

*2 oz. Absolut Los Angeles*

*1 oz. simple syrup (dissolve one part sugar in one part boiling water; let cool)*

*1 oz. lemon juice*

*1 spoonful of seedless blackberry jam*

*Splash of sparkling wine*

*Garnish: blackberries*

Put all ingredients except wine into a shaker, and shake vigorously. Strain over ice in a glass. Top with sparkling wine and blackberries.

**—The Volstead, New York City**

**COSMO TIP**

# Principispessa

1 ½ oz. Amaretto
1 ½ oz. Tuaca
1 oz. almond milk
Garnish: star anise

Mix all ingredients in a
cocktail shaker with ice,
and shake vigorously. Pour
into a chilled glass, and
top with star anise.

**—Eighty One, New York City**

# What Kind of Flirt Are You?

**1. You notice a gorgeous man standing in line behind you at the grocery store, so you:**

**a)** Pluck one of the bananas off a bunch, peel it *slooowly*, then take a bite.

**b)** Point to the tabloids and say, "Another train-wreck in Hollywood, huh?"

**c)** Check if he's wearing a ring, then glance away before he catches you.

**2. A hottie lifting weights at the gym is looking your way. How do you respond?**

**a)** Hiking up your shorts and pushing your butt way out as you do squats

**b)** Joking with him about how the StairMaster is a medieval torture device

**c)** Smiling then sniffing your shirt to check for BO

### 3. Stuck in a random city on a business trip, you do which of the following at the hotel restaurant?

**a)** Ask a good-looking guy at the bar if he'd mind showing you the must-see sites in town.

**b)** Get a table for two: you and your book. That way, you can still scope out the scene.

**c)** Nothing. You'll request the cutest waiter to deliver room service.

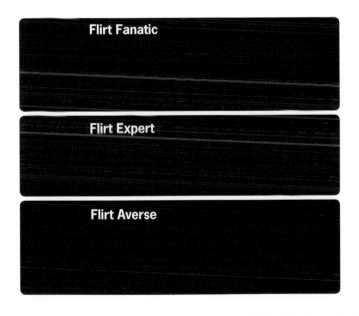

**Flirt Fanatic**

**Flirt Expert**

**Flirt Averse**

# CHAPTER 3

# Fearless & Fabulous

**When you're feeling bold,** you want a drink that matches your mood. These cocktails are big on flavor, use unexpected ingredients, and will put that extra pep in your step. Drink one to celebrate getting a promotion, asking a guy out…or any other badass move you've made lately. Knowing you, there have probably been more than a few!

# Berry Mojito

. . . . . . . . . . . . . .

5 fresh mint leaves
1 tsp. granulated sugar
4 lime wedges, juiced
2 oz. Bacardi Razz
¼ oz. Chambord
¼ oz. Blue Curaçao
Splash of club soda
Garnish: mint, blueberries, and raspberries

In a tall glass, crush mint with a fork. Add sugar and lime juice; stir. Add Bacardi, Chambord, and Blue Curaçao. Mix, and top with club soda. Garnish.

—*Chad Weller, Rumi, Miami*

### CONVO STARTER
This fruity beverage hails from Cuba. Since you're sipping something exotic, go around and have everyone name the tropical island they'd most like to visit.

# Strawberry Basil Margarita

1 oz. tequila
1 oz. triple sec
½ oz. Rose's Lime
2 oz. fresh strawberries with stems removed (or frozen strawberries)
1 fresh basil leaf, plus 1 for garnish
Garnish: lime slice

Blend all ingredients with ice. Garnish with slices of strawberry and lime and a basil leaf.

—*Eben Klemm, Dos Caminos, New York City*

**COSMO TIP** Keep your lipstick or gloss from coming off while you sip by licking the rim of the glass where you'll put your lips. The wetness allows your lips to slide over the glass instead of sticking and pulling off your makeup.

# Melon Mint Martini

1 sprig of fresh mint, plus 1 for garnish
2 Tbsp. cantaloupe
1 tsp. sugar

2 oz. vodka
1 oz. orange juice
Garnish: cantaloupe slice

In the bottom of a shaker, muddle mint, cantaloupe, and sugar. Add vodka, orange juice, and ice. Shake, and strain into a glass. Garnish with slice of cantaloupe and mint.

**—Quattro Gastronomia Italiana, Miami**

**HOOK-HIM HINT** Here's a move that will make any man melt while you're enjoying a drink with him: As you sip, make direct eye contact over the rim of your glass. When you lower the glass, slowly lick any leftover liquid from your lips.

PARTY FAVORITE!

# My Kurant Affair

2 oz. Absolut Kurant
¼ oz. cassis
1½ oz. lemon juice

Splash of club soda
½ oz. simple syrup
Garnish: fresh red grapes

Put all ingredients into a shaker with ice. Shake well. Strain into a chilled stemmed glass, and garnish with grapes. —*Hatfield's, Los Angeles*

## COSMO TIP

Even when you're armed with convo-starting current events from the newspaper, you don't want to seem like a know-it-all—that will make you seem, frankly, obnoxious. Being smart is an attribute, of course, but if you show off, it alienates your audience. So when you're trying to stoke a conversation with an interesting tidbit, couch your smarts in an unintimidating way. Introduce the topic by saying something like "I learned this cool thing recently...."

# The Sunroom Sinner

• • • • • • • • • • •

*1½ oz. dark rum*
*½ oz. chocolate liqueur*
*½ oz. Amaretto*
*Garnish: chocolate shavings*

Mix all ingredients in a shaker with ice, and strain into a glass. Garnish with chocolate shavings.

**—The Sunroom at The Water Club, Atlantic City**

**HOOK-HIM HINT** Be extra wicked while your guy is drinking this one. Lean in to him, and whisper a simply sinful thing you want to do to him. It'll be even naughtier if you do this while you're sitting in a room full of people.

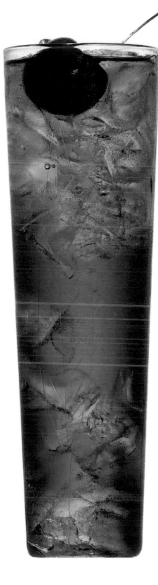

# Cherry Punch

• • • • • • • • • • • •

*1 oz. cherry vodka*
*1 oz. triple sec*
*Splash of Rose's Grenadine*
*Splash of cranberry juice*
*Garnish: fresh cherry*

Shake together vodka, triple sec, and grenadine with ice. Pour into a glass, and top with cranberry juice. Garnish with cherry.

**—Brooke Isaacson,
Club One, Baltimore**

**COSMO TIP** Sipping a tall drink slowly through a straw will draw attention to your lips—it's a move guys find totally sexy.

# Luxe Martini

*1 oz. Ketel One Citroen*
*½ oz. Chambord*
*¼ oz. Blue Curaçao*
*2 oz. white cranberry juice*
*Garnish: skewered cranberries*

Fill a cocktail shaker with ice. Add all ingredients, and shake well. Pour an extra splash of Blue Curaçao into the bottom of a martini glass, then strain mixture from shaker over top. Garnish with skewered cranberries.

**—Daniel Seelbinder,
Bar Luxe, Denver**

**COSMO TIP** Stand out by sporting a sparkly necklace or, hell, even a tiara. Wearing something unique gets the conversation going.

# Orange Sage

. . . . . . . . . . . . . . . . . . . . . .

1½ oz. Tanqueray No. Ten
3 fresh sage leaves, torn,
plus 1 for garnish

1½ oz. lime sour (combine
equal parts fresh lime juice
and sweet and sour mix)
½ oz. Alizé Gold Passion

Shake all ingredients with ice, then strain into a tumbler.
Garnish with fresh sage leaf.

**—Don Adams, Palomino, Seattle**

**COSMO TIP** Put on that million-dollar grin. When men see your
pearly whites, they automatically want to flash a smile back.

63

# Honeydew Margarita

1 oz. honeydew melon puree
1½ oz. tequila
1 oz. triple sec
¾ oz. fresh lime juice

½ oz. simple syrup (dissolve
one part sugar in one part
boiling water; let cool)
Salt (optional)
Garnish: skewered melon balls

Shake all ingredients with ice, and pour into a glass (salt
the rim if that's what you like). Garnish with melon balls.

**—Christopher Baljag, Plate, New York City**

**COSMO TIP** Make it a frozen margarita (as shown) by
throwing all the ingredients into a blender with a handful of
ice and blending until smooth. Or swap out the honeydew for
cantaloupe and you'll get a slightly sweeter concoction.

# The Firefly

2 oz. Absolut Citron
Splash of lemon juice
Splash of pineapple juice
½ oz. Midori Melon Liqueur
Garnish: 2 skewered
cherries

Put vodka, both juices,
and ice in a cocktail
shaker. Shake, and strain
into a martini glass. Then
add Midori, which will sink
to the bottom. Garnish
with skewered cherries.

**—Mojo, New York City**

**DID YOU KNOW?**
Fireflies glow at night
as part of their mating
ritual—their light-up
signals are timed in a
way that is meant to
attract the best mate.

# Cranberry Ginger Martini

. . . . . . . . . . . . . .

2 tsp. grated ginger
8 cranberries (fresh or frozen)
4 oz. cranberry vodka
Splash of lime juice
Splash of cranberry juice
Splash of simple syrup (dissolve one part sugar in one part boiling water; let cool)
Splash of Sprite
Garnish: lemon twist

Muddle ginger and cranberries in a shaker. Add ice, vodka, both juices, and simple syrup. Shake well. Strain into a martini glass, and add Sprite. Garnish with lemon twist.

**—The Fireplace,
Brookline, Massachusetts**

# Tequila Lime Granita Cocktail

*1 oz. tequila*
*1 oz. fresh lime juice*
*½ oz. sweet and sour mix*
*Lemon-lime soda*
*1 scoop lime granita or sorbet*
*Garnish: lime zest*

Chill a rocks glass in freezer, then add tequila, lime juice, and sweet and sour mix. Fill the rest of the glass with lemon-lime soda. Float the granita on top, and garnish with lime zest.

**—Chef J's Kitchen, Los Angeles**

**CONVO STARTER** While sipping these with the girls, play a game of Would You Rather? Kick it off with this question: Would you rather hook up with a pro athlete or a famous rock star?

**COSMO TIP** Multiply the ingredients by six and you'll have enough for a small pitcher to serve friends.

# Orange Splash

*2 oz. Absolut Citron*
*1 oz. Cointreau or triple sec*

*Splash each of fresh lime juice and orange juice*
*Garnish: orange slice*

Pour all ingredients over ice in a shaker, and shake vigorously. Rim a glass with sugar, and serve on the rocks. Garnish with slice of orange.

**—Shane Bachelor, Bar Twenty3, Nashville**

PARTY FAVORITE!

Cosmo's Official Cocktail Book

# The Fresh Sunrise

3 lemon wedges
1 tsp. sugar
4 oz. Alizé Bleu
Splash of sparkling wine, like prosecco
Garnish: lemon twist

Put lemon wedges in a shaker with sugar, and muddle.
Pour in Alizé Bleu, top with ice, and shake vigorously.
Then strain into a champagne flute, and top with sparkling wine. Garnish with lemon twist.

**—Delyn Hall and Bethany LaVoo, Fresh, New York City**

## CONVO STARTER
Here's a fun way to find out some juicy new info about your closest friends:
- Ask everyone to tell the story of the last time they watched a sunrise. When you're up that late (or that early!), there's usually a naughty reason.
- Have each person vote on whose story was the sexiest. Keep an extra bottle of prosecco on hand to award to the winner.
- Challenge everyone to beat the winner's sexy sunrise. Play again in a few weeks or months to see who has topped her story!

# Berry Burst

1½ oz. Belvedere
Black Raspberry
4 oz. skim milk
1 oz. heavy cream

6 strawberries
Garnish: fresh
blackberries

Put all ingredients in a blender (toss
in strawberries last), and add a handful
of crushed ice. Blend until smooth,
and pour into a glass. Garnish with
skewered blackberries.

—**Mixologist Claire Smith**

**CONVO STARTER**
This question will surely
spark a lively debate: Ask
everyone if they'd rather
date a guy with a great
booty or a killer six-pack.

# Aqua Loca

Chopped fruit
(whatever you
have on hand)
½ oz. rum
½ oz. vodka

½ oz. red wine
½ oz. white wine
½ oz. orange juice
½ oz. pineapple juice
½ oz. margarita mix

Place chopped fruit in the bottom of a
glass with ice. Add all ingredients, and stir.
Garnish with a slice of fruit.

—**Crema Restaurante, New York City**

**COSMO TIP** Construct a minibar on your
kitchen counter: Set out whatever alcohol and
mixers you have, and invite your friends to mix
up their own creation and even give it a name!

# Jalisco Flower Sangria

4 oz. Partida Blanco Tequila

6 oz. St-Germain

8 oz. pink grapefruit juice

1 bottle of prosecco

Garnish: slices of grapefruit, kiwi, and orange

Mix together all ingredients in a punch bowl or pitcher. Pour into glasses filled with ice.

**—Vincenzo Marianella, Copa d'Oro, Santa Monica**

## COSMO TIP

Place a pretty flower in your hair when you're serving this drink. Then, as you pour it, say "Try some Jalisco Flower Sangria"—you'll be totally festive.

# What Kind of Gutsy Are You?

**1.** If a guy is MIA a week after a great date, you:

**a)** Post "Hello— you still alive?" on his Facebook wall and text him for good measure.

**b)** Send a quick "Thought you'd get a kick out of this video" e-mail to show you're interested but not desperate.

**c)** Check your cell every five minutes and bum out over each "No missed calls" message.

**2.** Your roommate threw a party, and now your place looks like a war zone. What's your response?

**a)** Get the landlord to inform her that she can find a new place or face eviction.

**b)** Channel your rage into a text, telling her you'll discuss the situation in person.

**c)** Bitch about it to everyone but your roomie. She gets the silent treatment.

**3.** At a wedding, the band strikes up your favorite song as a superhot groomsman catches your eye. You:

**a)** Saunter over to him and say, "You. Me. Dance floor. Now."

**b)** Are the first to shake it, throwing some flirtatious glances his way.

**c)** Smile shyly at him before heading back to your table.

## MOSTLY As Way-Brave Babe

You stand your ground, even if it means trampling those who challenge you. But your arrogant MO can backfire—especially when it comes to guys. Instead of demanding things in such an inelegant way, try to figure out a way to respond calmly, directly, and respectfully. Stumped? Ask a pal how to tone it down. Focus less on being superior and you'll get what you want more often.

## MOSTLY Bs So-Gutsy Girl

You're so fearless, you just might belong on the cover of Cosmo! After all, who can resist a plucky chick who speaks her mind? You understand that rewards involve risk, and you get results because you're ambitious in a way that's still dignified. Keep practicing that courage, girl, and there will be no stopping you.

## MOSTLY Cs Shrinking Violet

Look in the mirror and ponder this: If you don't stick up for yourself, who will? In the event that someone doesn't hear you out when you say your piece, don't take it lying down. When facing a roomie who takes advantage of you, for example, have a response prepared. You don't need permission to show your badass side...all you need is the confidence to let it shine.

# CHAPTER 4

# A Little Romance

**Love is in the air...**or at least it will be after you and your sweetie taste these passionate potions. Make one to preface a gourmet dinner with your man; serve another on an occasion like your anniversary, his birthday, or hell, an ordinary Tuesday. Because almost any time's the right time for romance.

# Pink Eye

. . . . . . . . . . . . . . . .

*Half a lemon, cut into wedges*
*1½ oz. vodka*
*½ oz. triple sec*
*Splash of simple syrup*
*(dissolve one part sugar in one*
*part boiling water; let cool)*
*Sugar*
*¼ oz. Chambord*

Muddle lemon. Mix all ingredients but Chambord in a
shaker with ice. Shake, then
strain into a sugar-rimmed
glass. Pour Chambord down
side of glass. Garnish with
lemon twist.

**—John Hawkley, Cyclops, Seattle**

**HOOK-HIM HINT** While
drinking these, play a game
of Hangman. Draw a blank
space for every letter that
spells out your sentiment
("I love you" or "You're
amazing"), then make him
guess letters until he figures
out the message.

# Kerasi
## (Greek for *cherry*)

. . . . . . . . . .

*2 oz. peach vodka*
*1 oz. cherry puree (blend some fresh pitted cherries)*
*½ oz. peach liqueur*
*½ oz. cherry brandy*
*½ oz. lemon juice*
*Sparkling wine, like Cava*
*Garnish: cherry*

Shake all ingredients but the Cava over ice, and strain into a flute glass. Top with Cava. Garnish with cherry.

**—Philip Pepperdine,
Barbounia, New York City**

**HOOK-HIM HINT** Have your cutie hold your drink while you pull up your hair. Revealing your neck is irresistible to lots of men.

# Chocolate Martini

2 oz. vodka
1 tsp. vanilla extract
1 oz. Frangelico
4 oz. chilled hot chocolate

Combine all ingredients in a shaker with ice, shake, and pour into a stemmed glass. To make it even sweeter, dip the rim of the glass in honey and then in cookie crumbs.

—*7 Square Restaurant,*
*New York City*

**COSMO TIP** Serve this on an occasion when you want to feel extra romantic. The chocolate will make the event feel more decadent and special.

# Lemon-Drop Martini

· · · · · · · · · · · · ·

*1 oz. Absolut Citron*

*1 oz. limoncello*

*2 or 3 basil leaves, chopped, plus 1 more for garnish*

*2 squeezes of a lemon wedge, plus lemon slice for garnish*

Mix vodka, limoncello, basil, and juice in a shaker over ice. Shake, and strain into a chilled glass. Garnish with lemon slice and basil.

**—Arthur Greenan, One Sixtyblue, Chicago**

**COSMO TIP** Whenever you garnish with fruit, wash it before slicing. Even though you're not going to be eating the skin, it will touch your drink, so you want to make sure it's clean.

# Summer Sunset

. . . . . . . . . . . .

2 oz. vodka
Splash of triple sec
Splash of pomegranate
juice
Half a lemon
Garnish: cinnamon stick

Shake together all
ingredients with ice, then
strain into a chilled glass.
Garnish with cinnamon
stick or a slice of lemon.

**—Mixologist Adam Kane**

**COSMO TIP** Put your cocktail glasses in the freezer 10
minutes before you're ready to use them. They'll get perfectly
frosty and be able to keep your drinks cooler for longer.

PARTY FAVORITE!

Cosmo's Official Cocktail Book

# Black Crush

3 blackberries
6 mint leaves
½ oz. simple syrup (dissolve one part
sugar in one part boiling water; let cool)
1½ oz. Absolut Raspberri
1 oz. sour mix
Club soda

Muddle blackberries, mint, and simple syrup in a
shaker. Add vodka, sour mix, and ice. Strain into a
glass. Add a splash of club soda.

—*Sensi, Las Vegas*

## HOOK-HIM HINTS

Even if you know a guy well, you can always use insight into what he's thinking. Learn to read his lips!

● **If he smirks:** Even though it can look like a sneer, it means he wants to smile but is feeling self-conscious. A mini smile is a "controlled" grin.

● **If he covers his mouth with his palm:** Something's making him nervous. Shielding his lips shows he's feeling too tongue-tied to speak. Help him out!

● **If he bites his lip:** He's hot for you! Chewing is what we do to something that's yummy. Why not give him a few ideas?

# Ko Tao Sunset

. . . . . . . . . . . . . . . . . . . . .

1½ oz. vodka
½ oz. freshly squeezed lemon juice
¾ oz. honey
About 1 oz. club soda (depending on the size of the glass)
1 oz. pomegranate juice
Garnish: lemon slice

Put everything except the club soda and pomegranate juice in a shaker. Shake, and strain over ice. Add club soda and pomegranate juice. Garnish with slice of lemon.

**—Pranna, New York City**

# The Pink Ginger

. . . . . . . . . . . . . . . . . . . . .

1½ oz. Belvedere Pink Grapefruit

¼ oz. Domaine de Canton Liqueur

¼ oz. lime juice

½ oz. cranberry juice

Splash of sweet and sour mix

Garnish: pink grapefruit zest or slice

Pour all liquid ingredients into a shaker with ice, and shake. Pour into a glass, and garnish with strips of grapefruit zest or a slice of grapefruit.　**—Mixologist Claire Smith**

**HOOK-HIM HINT** Drink your cocktail with a straw. This will bring extra attention to your luscious pout.

# The Poinsettia

. . . . . . . . . . . . . . . . . .

½ oz. Grand Marnier
4 oz. champagne
Splash of cranberry juice
Garnish: 3 dried cranberries

Pour the Grand Marnier
into the bottom of a tall
flute. Then pop the cork
on the champagne, and fill
the glass. Before serv-
ing, top with cranberry
juice and float a few dried
cranberries on top.

—*Forge, New York City*

**COSMO TIP** There's
something romantic about
champagne—maybe
it's the elegance of the
flutes. So to make a night
special, go for a drink
with some bubbly. You'll
transform the mood.

# Sweet Red Kiss

. . . . . . . . . . . . . . .

1½ oz. Dubonnet Rouge
⅓ oz. Chambord
⅓ oz. Absolut Kurant
Splash each of orange, pineapple, and cranberry juices
Sugar
Garnish: orange and pineapple chunks

Shake all liquid ingredients with ice. Strain into a sugar-rimmed glass. Garnish with orange and pineapple.

—*James Michael Bobby, Kumo Restaurant, West Hollywood*

**DID YOU KNOW?** Something for you and your husband to think about: Men who kiss their wives every morning reportedly live five years longer than those who don't.

# Pink Margarita

. . . . . . . . . . . . . . . . . . . . . . . . . .

1½ oz. tequila          ¼ oz. Campari
½ oz. fresh lemon juice     ½ oz. honey
*Garnish: lemon slice and mint leaf*

Put all ingredients into a cocktail shaker with
ice, and shake vigorously. Serve on the rocks,
and garnish with slice of lemon and mint.

**—James Stuart, Parea, New York City**

**COSMO TIP** You need only three to six ice
cubes in the shaker to chill this drink perfectly.

# White Ginger

. . . . . . . . . . . . . . . . . . . .

*Crushed gingersnaps*
*¼ oz. Cointreau*
*¼ tsp. grated ginger*
*1¼ oz. Hangar One Citron*
*1 oz. white cranberry juice*

Wet the rim of a glass, and dip it into the crushed cookies. Muddle the Cointreau and ginger in a shaker. Add remaining ingredients with ice, shake, and pour.

**—First Food & Bar at The Palazzo, Las Vegas**

**COSMO TIP** On date night, while you sip your drinks, go through your most recent issue of Cosmo and pick out the sexy stuff you'd like to try together.

# The Delancey

. . . . . . . . . . . . . . . . . . . .

¾ oz. pomegranate
juice
¾ oz. St-Germain
Prosecco

Mix together the juice
and liqueur, and pour
into a champagne flute.
Top with prosecco.

**—Richard H. Friedberg, Allen
and Delancey, New York City**

## HOOK-HIM HINT
Drinking with a new
guy? Do something to
initiate physical contact,
such as "reading" his
palm. As you trace the
lines, tell him you see
that he'll live a long life.

PARTY FAVORITE!

Cosmo's Official Cocktail Book

# The Passion Daiquiri

. . . . . . . . . . . . . . . . . . . . .

1 oz. rum
⅔ oz. vanilla liqueur
1½ oz. passion-fruit juice
½ cup water
⅓ oz. simple syrup (dissolve one part sugar
in one part boiling water; let cool)

Place all ingredients in a blender. Add a
handful of ice cubes, and blend until it has a
smoothie-like consistency.

**—Ken Oringer, Clio Restaurant, Boston**

## DID YOU KNOW?

If you and your guy have been together for a while, PDA doesn't have to be a thing of the past. Being public about your love is essential to keeping your connection solid and sex percolating. Of course, most displays are better left behind closed doors, but don't be afraid to make out at a party or exchange sexy eyes across the table during a date. Having to stay within parameters when you're around others adds playfulness and excitement that you can bring back to the bedroom later.

# Twinkle Toes

· · · · · · · ·

1 oz. Stoli Vanil
1 oz. pear nectar (or juice)
½ oz. agave nectar
2 oz. champagne

Put everything into a glass with ice. Stir well, and serve.

**—Mixologist Charlotte Voisey**

### HOOK-HIM HINT
According to body-language experts, a guy's more likely to approach you if your feet are less than 6 inches apart and your toes are pointed slightly inward.

# Solerno Bellini

- - - - - - - - - - - - -

1 oz. Solerno Blood
Orange Liqueur

3 oz. blood orange puree

3 oz. prosecco

Combine everything in a
mixing glass in order of
ingredients list. Add ice,
stir, and strain into a flute.

**—Gramercy Park Hotel,
New York City**

### DID YOU KNOW?
This cocktail is named
after artist Giovanni
Bellini because in one of
his paintings, someone
is drinking a beverage
of this color.

91

# Where Do You Rate on the Passion Scale?

**1.** The most impulsive thing you can imagine doing (or have done) with a guy is:

**a)** Moving in together within your first month of meeting.

**b)** Going on a trip with him after just two weeks of dating.

**c)** Drunk-dialing him.

**2.** Is it possible for you to be in love with two guys at once?

**a)** Of course—it's not always possible to control whom you fall for, after all.

**b)** Probably not. You pretty much choose to get emotionally involved with one man at a time.

**c)** No way. You fully give a guy your head and your heart.

**3.** When you and a guy disagree on something, you:

**a)** Refuse to back down, even if you create more drama than Real Housewives do.

**b)** Get a kick out of pushing his buttons but stay respectful of his views.

**c)** Drop the subject—conflict is not an aphrodisiac.

**4.** When it comes to achieving your goals, you:

**a)** Pity the fool who tries to stop you from getting what you want.

**b)** Aim high and revise downward if necessary.

**c)** Set the bar low-ish—who wants to be disappointed?

### MOSTLY As Go-to-Extremes Girl

Hot damn, you're a fiery one! You're consumed by the thrill of new experiences and relationships, but because you're so intense, your enthusiasm often flames out quickly. Shacking up ASAP or devoting yourself to a new guy 24/7 may feel exciting, but consider if these things go along with your long-term goals.

### MOSTLY Bs Balanced Passionista

Fortune favors the brave, and baby, you've hit the jackpot! You don't let fear keep you from embarking on an adventure, such as taking a vacation with a new guy. And you're levelheaded enough that if the experience doesn't live up to your hopes, you're not disappointed for long—you're already on to the next big thing.

### MOSTLY Cs Too-Tempered Chick

You may have been taught that polite women aren't audacious or rash...but they aren't seen as a hell of a lot of fun either. So here's your permission to boldly go after what you want: Pursue guys you feel a real spark with, not just the ones you feel comfortable with. In love, it's never a good idea to settle for safe.

# CHAPTER 5

# Sweet Seduction

**The best way to describe** the following pages of spirits? Sexy and damn delicious. If you're trying to tempt a new man or are looking for fresh ways to turn on the guy you have, just serve him one of these and have some lusty activities up your sleeve, you'll seal the deal, guaranteed.

# Sea Spray Kiss

· · · · · · · · ·

1 oz. pear vodka

8 raspberries

½ oz. Chambord

½ oz. simple syrup
(dissolve one part
sugar in one part boiling
water; let cool)

3 oz. prosecco

Mash raspberries
with simple syrup and
Chambord in a shaker,
then add vodka and
ice; shake well. Strain
into a glass, and
top with prosecco.

—*The Penthouse,
Santa Monica*

**DID YOU KNOW?**
Your lips are packed
with nerve endings,
which is what makes
kissing feel *soo* good.

# Forbidden Fruit

· · · · · · · · ·

*2 oz. Absolut Mandrin*

*1 oz. crème de banana liqueur*

*1 oz. Midori Melon Liqueur*

*1 oz. sour mix*

*Garnish: strawberry and apple slice*

Put all ingredients in a shaker, add ice, and shake. Strain into a cocktail glass. Garnish with strawberry and slice of apple.

**—Tom Fuls, Blue Martini, Raleigh, North Carolina**

**COSMO TIP** Ask your boyfriend what made him notice you for the first time, and share what initially drew you to him, too.

# Dancing With the Devil

1½ oz. tequila
½ oz. Chambord
½ oz. freshly squeezed
lime juice

Splash of ginger beer
Garnish: crystallized ginger
or lime wedge

Pour tequila, Chambord, and lime juice into a glass. Add ice,
and stir. Top with ginger beer. Garnish with crystallized ginger or
a lime wedge.

**—BLT Burger, Las Vegas**

**COSMO TIP** Play some sexy tunes while sipping this drink (think
Ray LaMontagne or Marvin Gaye). Who knows? After one or two,
you just may be inspired to turn your living room into a dance floor.

PARTY FAVORITE!

# Saba Colada

. . . . . . . . . . . . . . . . . . . . . . . . . . . .

*2 oz. Malibu rum*
*2 Tbsp. Thai coconut milk*
*3 Tbsp. pineapple juice*
*3 Tbsp. simple syrup (dissolve one part sugar*
*in one part boiling water; let cool)*
*Splash of Blue Curaçao*
*Garnish: coconut slice*

Blend rum, milk, juice, and syrup with ice on high until foamy. Add Curaçao, and top with slice of coconut.

**—Nate Wales, Saba Blue Water Café, Austin**

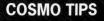

**COSMO TIPS**

# Naughty Girl Scout

· · · · · · · · · · · · · · · · · · · · · · · · · · · · ·

*2 oz. Kahlúa*
*1 oz. crème de menthe*

*1 oz. half-and-half*
*Garnish: mint leaves*

Fill a cocktail shaker with ice. Add ingredients, shake well, and pour over ice. Garnish with mint leaves.

—*Arturo Gomez, Rockit Bar & Grill, Chicago*

**HOOK-HIM HINT**

# Frozen Bellini

. . . . . . . . . . . . .

2½ oz. sparkling wine

1 oz. triple sec

1 oz. peach puree
(blend a ripe peach)

1 oz. simple syrup
(dissolve one part sugar
in one part boiling
water; let cool) plus a
squeeze of lemon

Garnish: peach wedge

Blend all ingredients
with ice. Garnish with
peach wedge.

**—Guido Ortuno,
Chaya Brasserie,
Los Angeles**

**COSMO TIP**

# Watermelon Julep

· · · · · · · · · ·

¼ ripe watermelon

½ oz. simple syrup (dissolve
one part sugar in one part
boiling water; let cool)

3 sprigs of rosemary

2 oz. Grey Goose vodka

Smash watermelon until it is
juice. Remove seeds. Muddle
2 sprigs of rosemary with
syrup. Add 3 oz. watermelon
juice and vodka, and shake
with ice. Strain, and garnish
with sprig of rosemary.

**—Myles Atherton, Irving Mill,
New York City**

**COSMO TIP**

# The Tramonto

. . . . . . . . . . . . . . . . . . . . .

1½ oz. tequila
¾ oz. Aperol
½ oz. Solerno Blood
Orange Liqueur

¾ oz. grapefruit juice
2 dashes of orange bitters
Garnish: orange twist

Shake together everything in a shaker, and strain into a cocktail glass. Garnish with orange twist.

**—Locanda Verde, New York City**

**HOOK-HIM HINT** Let some of your drink dribble onto your lips, then tell your guy you'd like him to lick it off. He gets bonus points if he uses his tongue in an imaginative way.

PARTY FAVORITE!

# Passion Fruit Caipiroska

. . . . . . . . . . . . . . . . . . . . . . . .

2 oz. passion fruit juice

1 oz. simple syrup (dissolve one part sugar
in one part boiling water; let cool)

2 oz. Absolut vodka

1 oz. lime juice

½ oz. lemon juice

Put all ingredients in a shaker, and shake together.
Strain into a large stemmed glass, and garnish with
something fun, like a bright flower.

—*Colin Campbell, BLT Steak, Washington, D.C.*

## DID YOU KNOW?

Scientists recently discovered that there's a big gap between what men watch and what they want in reality. So don't worry too much if he's into porn; it doesn't change the type of sex he wants to have with you—what he's eyeing on his laptop is likely just fantasy. Speaking of what dudes want, here are their top picks for outdoor sex locales that you may want to make a reality for him:

- 33% say in a pool.
- 30% say on a beach.
- 23% say by a campfire.
- 14% say in a hammock

# The Burning Mandarin

. . . . . . . . . . . . . . . . . . . . . . . . . . . . . . . . .

*2 slices of serrano chili pepper*
*1½ oz. Absolut Mandrin*
*½ oz. orange juice*
*¾ oz. fresh lemon juice*

*½ oz. simple syrup (dissolve one part sugar in one part boiling water; let cool)*
*½ oz. cranberry juice*

Muddle chili slices. Add the rest of the ingredients and ice. Shake, and strain into a glass. Garnish with extra peppers.

**—SBE's Katsuya Hollywood**

**COSMO TIP**

# The Pink Pussycat

Colored sugar
½ oz. Bombay Sapphire Gin
½ oz. pineapple juice
¾ oz. freshly squeezed grapefruit juice
Splash of grenadine

Wet the edge of a stemmed glass with a damp paper towel, and dip the glass in colored sugar. Then pour all ingredients over ice, and stir well. **—The Smith, New York City**

# Rosy Sangria

½ bottle of Rosangel tequila
½ bottle of white wine
1 oz. orange juice
2 oz. cranberry juice
½ cup sugar
2 oranges, 1 lemon, and 1 lime, sliced
1 bunch of grapes, halved
1 apple, diced
½ liter club soda

Mix all ingredients in a large pitcher, and stir. When serving, make sure each glass gets some fruit chunks. **—Izzi Olmos, Boca Grande, Jersey City**

**COSMO TIP**

# Sake Julep

· · · · · · · · · ·

Mint leaf
½ tsp. sugar
½ ripe peach, diced
1½ oz. sake
1 oz. vodka
1½ oz. fresh lime juice
Tonic

Muddle mint and sugar in a cocktail shaker. Add peach; muddle again. Pour in sake; shake. Add vodka, lime juice, and ice; shake again. Strain over ice; top with tonic. Stir in extra peach chunks.

**—Bao 111, New York City**

**HOOK-HIM HINT** To create a more seductive ambience, drape scarves over your lamps or lightbulbs—they cast a softer glow than normal bulbs do.

# Spiced-Apple Martini

· · · · · · · · · · · ·

*2 oz. Captain
Morgan Spiced Rum*

*2 oz. sour-apple mix*

*Splash of
pineapple juice*

*Garnish: apple slice*

Pour all ingredients
over ice, and shake.
Strain into a martini
glass, and garnish.

**—Landmarc,
New York City**

Cosmo's Official Cocktail Book

# Periodista
## ("The Journalist")

. . . . . . . . . . . . . . . . . . . . . . . . .

*Juice of half a lime, plus 1 slice for garnish*
*1 tsp. sugar*
*Splash of apricot brandy*
*½ cup apricot pureo (blend fresh apricots)*
*Splash of triple sec*
*1½ oz. Bacardi Superior*
*Garnish: skewered dried apricots*

Shake all ingredients over ice, then strain into a glass.
Garnish with skewered dried apricots and slice of lime.

**—Douglas Rodriguez, Ola, Miami**

**COSMO TIPS**

# Agave Stinger

. . . . . . . . . . . . . . . . . . . . . . . .

1 oz. honey
2 oz. tequila
1 oz. fresh lime juice

2 dashes of bitters
Splash of soda

Heat the honey on low. Once it's dark amber, remove from heat. Mix everything but the soda in a shaker. Pour over ice. Top with soda.

**—Alex Fathalla, Commerce, New York City**

**DID YOU KNOW?** Wearing 2-inch heels may improve the strength of your pelvic muscles, which helps you orgasm. Just another reason to sport those pumps!

# Polar Razz

. . . . . . . . . .

2 oz. raspberry
vodka

1 oz. triple sec

1 oz. lime juice

3 oz. whole raspberries
(fresh or frozen)

Blend all ingredients
with ice. Garnish with
raspberries or any
striking exotic fruit.

—*Laura Maniec, J Bar,*
*Scottsdale, Arizona*

**COSMO TIP**

**COSMO QUIZ**

# Are You Good-Girl Hot or Bad-Girl Hot?

**1. You spot a cute guy across the room at a party, and the pleasure center of your brain instantly lights up. You:**

**a)** Stroll right over and whisper "Need another drink?" while his is still full.

**b)** "Accidentally" brush up against him, smile, and introduce yourself.

**c)** Stay put until he finally chats with a mutual friend, then make your move.

**2. After spending the evening deep in conversation with a new dude, you usually end up:**

**a)** Pulling him into the bathroom for a steamy make-out session.

**b)** Leaning in first to give him a quick good-night peck on the cheek.

**c)** Waiting for him to kiss you, then sending him a flirty text after you part ways.

## 3. Most of the guys you've dated would probably best describe you as:

**a)** The closest they'll ever come to Angelina Jolie...in her bicurious knife-play phase.

**b)** The craziest girl they've been with in bed whom they could still bring home to meet the parents.

**c)** The kind of woman with whom they try to remain friends (without benefits) after the breakup.

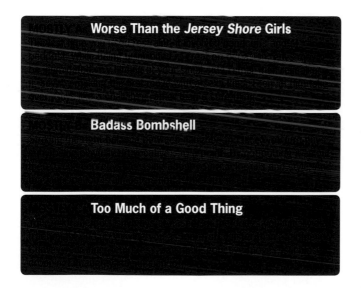

**Worse Than the _Jersey Shore_ Girls**

**Badass Bombshell**

**Too Much of a Good Thing**

# CHAPTER 6

# What a Guy Wants

**Nothing froufrou or girlie here.**
These babies go down smooth—
which is why they appeal to men.
So call him up and ask him over
to your place. Then put on something smokin', dim the lights, and
mix up one of these cocktails—
whichever recipe you choose, it'll
bring new meaning to the words
"nice stiff drink."

# Spicy Peach

2 thin slices of serrano
chili pepper

A few lime slices

2 oz. Stoli Peachik

Splash of Rose's Lime

Splash of simple syrup
(dissolve one part
sugar in one part boiling
water; let cool)

Muddle chili-pepper slices
and lime in a shaker. Add ice,
vodka, Rose's Lime, and
simple syrup. Shake, and
strain into a stemmed glass.

**—Sam Fowler, Olive or Twist,
Portland, Oregon**

**CONVO STARTER** A fun
way to get a guy chatting:
Ask him which superhero he'd
want to be. It's a not-too-
personal question that he
won't mind opening up about.

# Cactus Pear Margarita

*2 oz. tequila*
*1 oz. Cointreau or triple sec*
*1 oz. cactus pear syrup*
*½ oz. lime juice*
*Garnish: lime and cactus pear slices*

Shake all ingredients in a shaker with ice for 10 seconds. Strain into a chilled glass with a salted rim; add garnish.

**—Laurence Kretchmer,
Mesa Grill, Las Vegas**

**HOOK-HIM HINT** Say "Damn. You've got a hot ass." Men crave reassurance about their appearance just like we do. Singling out a hot zone like his butt will make him feel objectified—in a good way.

# Coffee Frappe

. . . . . . . . . . . . . . . . . . . .

1½ cups cold water
1½ tsp. instant coffee
2 tsp. sugar

½ to 1 shot ouzo
Milk, vanilla ice cream,
chocolate syrup, and mint

Blend briefly 5 Tbsp. water, coffee, and sugar. Pour into a glass. Add ouzo, milk, ice, and remaining water. Top with ice cream, chocolate syrup, and mint.

—*Alki Stathopoulos, Kellari Taverna, New York City*

**COSMO TIP** This cocktail is a great substitute for a Bloody Mary if you're having your guy over for brunch. You'll get your caffeine fix *and* the pep of a cocktail.

PARTY FAVORITE!

Cosmo's Official Cocktail Book

# Pumpkin Ginger Martini

1-inch cube of ginger
1 tsp. unrefined sugar
2 oz. maple syrup
2 tsp. canned pumpkin puree
¾ oz. lemon juice
2 oz. Agua Luca

Muddle ginger and sugar in a shaker. Add other ingredients, shake, and strain into a glass.
—*Barmarché, New York City*

## DID YOU KNOW?

Every relationship has a balance of power that experts describe as the pursuer/distancer dynamic. The pursuer craves connection; the distancer requires greater emotional space. It's no surprise that women are usually the pursuers, but you *can* turn the tables. If you're often the one pushing for a tighter bond, detach a bit—hang out with friends more, take up a solo hobby, refrain from texting him as much. As you cool off, he'll warm up!

# Espresso Martini

· · · · · · · · · · · · ·

*Shot of espresso*
*½ oz. chocolate vodka*
*½ oz. Godiva Original Liqueur*
*¼ oz. Amaretto*
*¼ oz. Kahlúa*
*Milk-chocolate bar*
*Garnish: Baileys, whipped cream, and cocoa*

Shake ingredients with ice. Rim the glass with milk-chocolate bits (use a vegetable peeler to shave pieces from a candy bar). Strain into glass, and top with Baileys, whipped cream, and cocoa.

**—David Feuer, Deco, Houston**

**HOOK-HIM HINT** Both coffee and chocolate are yummy aphrodisiacs, so serve this with chocolate-covered espresso beans, and enjoy!

# The Apple-Disiac

. . . . . . . . . . . . . . . . . . . . . . . . . . . . . . . . . . .

1 oz. apple vodka
½ oz. coffee liqueur
1 oz. apple cider

Splash of cream
Garnish: apple slice

Mix all ingredients with ice in a shaker, and shake well. Strain into a glass. Garnish with slice of apple.

—*The Water Club, Atlantic City*

**CONVO STARTER** Watch his reaction to this: Ask him if he'd rather do the deed while tied up or blindfolded.

# Sparkling Screwdriver

. . . . . . . . . . . . . . . . . . . .

*1½ oz. Stoli vodka*
*A few orange slices*
*Splash of Perrier*

Fill a glass with ice, and add the orange slices (you can substitute blood oranges if you'd like). Pour in the vodka, then top with a splash of Perrier.

**—Zaré at Fly Trap, San Francisco**

**HOOK-HIM HINT** When a new guy asks for your info, forget the BBM exchange. Instead, grab your waterproof eyeliner from your bag and write your digits on his hand. According to our Web poll, 54% of guys say this move is super sexy.

# Stout Float

• • • • • • • • • •

3 or 4 scoops of vanilla ice cream

Bottle of oatmeal stout

Scoop ice cream into glass, and pour the bottle of stout over it. Serve. As a variation, try using other ice cream and stout flavors, such as strawberry ice cream and a blueberry brew.

**—Bill's Bar & Burger,
New York City**

**COSMO TIP** Give him a beer facial! First, wash his face. Then mix one egg white with ½ cup beer. Massage onto his skin, and wait 15 minutes. Remove with a warm, wet cloth.

# The Cuban

. . . . . . . . . . . . . . . . . . . . . . . . . . . .

*6 or 7 basil leaves*
*3 lime wedges, plus juice of half a lime*
*1 tsp. brown sugar*
*6 oz. light rum*
*Splash of tonic*

In a shaker, muddle basil, lime wedges, brown sugar, and juice of half a lime. Add rum and ice, and mix together. Pour into glass, and add a splash of tonic. Garnish with any extra basil.

*—Le Miu, New York City*

## COSMO TIP

Did he (or you) drink too much last night? Here's how to combat that pesky hangover:

● **Sleep in.** You'll recover faster if you can get at least six hours of sleep.

● **Drink a full glass of water** or two every hours.

● **Pop two aspirin** every four hours, but avoid acetaminophens (such as Tylenol) and NSAIDS (like Advil and Aleve).

● **Wear sunglasses.** Bright light prolongs head pain, so sporting shades can help cut a headache short.

● **Walk briskly for 20 minutes** to boost your metabolism and help you recover.

# The Ginger Man

. . . . . . . . . . . . . . . . . . . . . . . .

*1 oz. Hendrick's Gin*
*½ oz. ginger liqueur*
*Juice of half a lemon*
*2 oz. sparkling wine*
*Garnish: raspberry*

Mix gin, ginger liqueur, and
lemon juice in a shaker with ice.
Shake well. Strain into a tall
glass. Top with sparkling wine.
Garnish with raspberry.

—**Forty Eight, New York City**

**COSMO TIP** You can use any gin
you have in your cabinet, but the
Hendrick's adds a special kick of
flavor because it includes notes
of rose and cucumber.

# Mixed
# Berry
# Collins

1½ oz. Milagro Reposado Tequila
1 oz. Lillet Rouge
4 mint leaves

6 blackberries
4 oz. agave nectar
Garnish: sprig of rosemary

Muddle 5 blackberries in the bottom of a shaker. Add all other
ingredients, and shake well. Strain into a chilled glass filled with
crushed ice. Garnish with a blackberry and rosemary.

—*Mixologist Charlotte Voisey*

**HOOK-HIM HINT** Trying to get your crush to open up? Sit next
to him on the couch, and look around at the room. Guys feel more
comfortable revealing info if they're not making eye contact.

# Rum Punch

. . . . . . . . . . . .

2½ oz. light rum
4 oz. orange juice
4 oz. pineapple juice
Juice of 1 lime
*Garnish: maraschino
cherries and orange
slices*

Pour rum and
juices into a cocktail
shaker filled with
ice. Shake vigor-
ously for 10 to 15
seconds. Strain
into two glasses
filled with ice.
Garnish with cherries
and orange slices.

**—Katie Lee,**
***Cosmo food columnist***

**CONVO STARTER** This drink is sure to conjure up tropical-vacation
memories. Take turns telling each other about the best beach trips
you've ever taken. Then start planning one together.

# Frostbite

• • • • • • • • • • • • •

1 oz. Milagro Silver Tequila
½ oz. white crème de cacao
1 oz. cream
Garnish: grated chocolate

Put everything in a shaker
with ice. Shake well, and
strain into a glass. Top
with a sprinkle of grated
chocolate.

**—Mixologist Charlotte Voisey**

**DID YOU KNOW?** Silver
or blanco is the least
expensive tequila because
it hasn't been aged at all.
Reposado is the next level
up—it's been aged for
two months, so it's a little
more complex in taste.

# Cilantro Lime Soda

. . . . . . . . .

A few lime wedges

4 to 6 sprigs of cilantro

Splash of simple syrup
(dissolve one part
sugar in one part boiling
water; let cool)

2 oz. vodka

Soda water

Muddle limes, cilantro,
and simple syrup in the
bottom of a glass. Add
ice, vodka, and enough
soda water to fill the
glass. Stir to mix. Garnish
with a sprig of cilantro.

—*Cafeteria, New York City*

**COSMO TIP** Cilantro is often used in Mexican cuisine, so serve these with chips and salsa. Put on some mariachi music to complete the vibe.

# Peach Mai Tai

. . . . . . . . . . . . . .

*4 peach slices*

*½ oz. Myers's Rum*

*¼ oz. simple syrup (dissolve one part sugar in one part boiling water; let cool)*

*1 oz. Bacardi Peach Red*

*1 oz. triple sec*

*½ oz. lime juice*

*¼ oz. crème de noyaux*

In a shaker, muddle 3 peach slices with simple syrup. Add ice and everything else. Shake, and strain into a glass. Garnish with peach slice.

**—*The Continental, Atlantic City***

**CONVO STARTER** Single? Over this cocktail, ask your guy pals what they envision your dream man being like. Hearing from them may help you decide what you want.

PARTY FAVORITE!

Cosmo's Official Cocktail Book

# Jalapeño Margarita

3 jalapeño slices
2 cucumber slices
1 Tbsp. agave nectar
2 oz Cointreau
2½ oz. silver tequila

Juice of half a lime
Kosher salt

Muddle 1 jalapeño slice and 1 cucumber slice into agave nectar in a shaker; add liquor and lime juice. Shake, then strain into a salt-rimmed glass. Garnish with jalapeño and cucumber slices.

—**Lonesome Dove, Fort Worth, Texas**

## COSMO TIPS

You can learn a lot about a guy from the way he holds his drink. What to look for:

● **If he grips it loosely,** he feels in control of the situation. This could also be a bit of cocky posturing.

● **If he keeps it by his chest,** it's like a wall he's putting up. Stick to superficial topics until you sense him getting comfy.

● **If he pushes his glass toward you,** he's feeling the urge to bond. Men put stuff in your space when they want to get closer to you.

# The Tiger Paw

· · · · · · ·

*1 oz. raspberry wine
(such as Bonny Doon
Framboise) or Chambord*

*1 oz. Southern Comfort*

*1 oz. pineapple juice*

*Garnish: fruit slice
or lemon twist*

Put all ingredients into a cocktail shaker or pint glass. Add ice, then cover, shake, and strain into a martini glass. Garnish with a slice of fruit or lemon twist.

**—Jacques-Imo's,
New Orleans**

**HOOK-HIM HINT**
Ask him point-blank, "What's your secret erotic fantasy?"

# Smashing Pumpkin

. . . . . . . . . . . . . . . . . . . . . . . . . . . .

2 oz. Stoli Vanil
1 Tbsp. pumpkin puree
1 oz. cream

1 tsp. simple syrup (dissolve one part sugar in one part boiling water; let cool)
Garnish: cinnamon stick

Put everything into a cocktail shaker. Add ice, and shake. Pour into a glass over ice, and garnish with cinnamon stick.

**—BLT Steak, Washington, D.C.**

**CONVO STARTER** Pose this question when you serve this drink: "What was your most outrageous Halloween costume?" You'll know right away that he has a great sense of humor if he's worn some kooky getups.

# The Cosmo Quiz:
# Would You Rather...?

*Getting to know each other doesn't have to involve long, drawn-out conversations. Instead, pick your answers below, and have him do the same. Your responses will reveal quite a bit about both of you.*

## WOULD YOU RATHER...

...order an appetizer?  **OR**  ...order dessert?

**What your answer says about you:**

### APPETIZER
You don't feel the need to rush to the entrée, and the same holds true in your relationships. Instead of thinking about milestones you should be reaching, you stay in the moment.

### DESSERT
You savor a boyfriend or girlfriend the same way you do a piece of cake: by taking in and appreciating everything that makes that person special to you. Delicious.

## WOULD YOU RATHER...

...go on an adventurous trip?    **OR**    ...veg out at a tropical resort?

### What your answer says about you:

**TRIP**
You want someone who's up for trying new things, like eating ice cream at 3 a.m. or spending the day at an arcade.

**RESORT**
You feel that a calm atmosphere is of the utmost importance. You are always levelheaded and don't let drama rule your life.

## WOULD YOU RATHER...

...make a phone call?    **OR**    ...send a text?

### What your answer says about you:

**PHONE CALL**
You take time to let your significant other know you care. You'd much rather go out for a quiet dinner so you can talk than head to a trendy new club.

**TEXT**
You feel confident about doing and saying what comes to mind in the moment— you don't have any problems communicating freely with your partner.

## WOULD YOU RATHER...

...be a celebrity?    **OR**    ...be a well-known author?

### What your answer says about you:

**CELEBRITY**
You live for grandiose, straight-from-a-movie romantic gestures and prefer to show your love through things like flowers and unexpected gifts.

**AUTHOR**
You want the other person to consider you invaluable. Words are important—you hope your loved one can describe what he or she loves so much about you.

# The Cosmo Couples Quiz

*Whip up a few cocktails of your choice, then get started with this revealing game. First, write down your answers to the "She Asks" questions, and have him write down his answers to the "He Asks" questions. Then see if each of you can guess how the other responded.*

**If you both get at least seven right, you're enviably fused!**

## SHE ASKS, HE ANSWERS

1. Where's my ideal vacation spot?
2. Who's my closest friend?
3. Who's my celebrity crush?
4. What's my least favorite food?
5. What ice cream flavor do I crave the most?
6. Where were we the first time we had sex?
7. What's my favorite gift you've ever given me?
8. What form of exercise do I enjoy above all others?
9. Which of my body parts do I like the most?
10. What genre of movie do I usually want to watch?

### HE ASKS, SHE ANSWERS

1. What do I see myself doing in 10 years?
2. If forced, would I rather be made to dance or sing in public?
3. Who's my celebrity crush?
4. If I had to switch jobs with one of my friends, who would it be?
5. How do I like my steak done?
6. What genre of movie do I usually want to watch?
7. Which of my body parts do I like the most?
8. Who in my family do I call first with good news?
9. Would I pick fame or fortune?
10. Where am I more comfortable: in the city or the country?

**COUPLES BONUS: THE COSMO PASSION GAME**

# Suss Out His Fantasies

*Over drinks, get your guy to give you his erotic answers for the blanks below. Then read him the sexy finished product.*

It's _____ [time of day], and we're at _____ [location not traditionally associated with sex]. You lean in to me and whisper, "You look even hotter than _____ [sexy female celebrity]." Hearing the compliment makes me need you right now, so we decide to find some privacy ASAP. Once we're alone, we quickly strip. You grab a _____ [household object] and rub it seductively against my _____ [body part]. Inspired by how turned on I get, you head to the refrigerator to grab some _____ [gooey edible substance], which I slowly lick off your _____ [body part]. We then have wild sex for _____ [period of time], switching from _____ [sex position/move] to _____ [sex position/move] before we climax simultaneously. Afterward, we _____ [your favorite activity besides sex].

# Everything You Need for Your At-Home Bar

And your guy thinks his toolbox is cool.

## BAR SPOON

A bar spoon has an elongated handle with a twisted middle section and either a flat-disk or rounded end. Both ends are effective for stirring cocktails, while the twisted middle section lets you stir faster. Also, the spoon is equivalent to roughly a teaspoon, so it's great for measuring small amounts. One more thing: When you stir a drink, be gentle with the ice—aggressive stirring can break it up and dilute your drink, affecting its taste.

## BLENDER

This will be the most expensive piece of equipment in your basic bartending toolkit. A blender is the best route to all things frozen as well as a shortcut to chopping fruit when you don't have the time. Ice should always be the last ingredient you add to the blender—its weight will keep your ingredients close to the blade and make for an even blend. Whenever possible, use crushed ice as opposed to cubes, since it's easier on your blender.

## COCKTAIL SHAKER

You can get either a traditional cocktail shaker with a built-in strainer or a Boston shaker kit. The kit includes a tumbler that resembles a milkshake can and is usually made of stainless steel—meaning it is easy to keep clean and should stand the test of time—plus a mixing glass, which looks like a pint glass. The tumbler fits snugly over the mixing glass, forming a vacuum seal, so you can shake up your cocktail without any liquid leaking out. Tip: When cold, metal shakers can constrict, making it hard to separate the components; a gentle knock on the side of the shaker should break the seal.

## MEASURE/JIGGER

Always use a measure to make sure your cocktails have a consistent balance. You probably see some bartenders pouring by sight, but that method takes a long time to perfect. So, literally, don't try it at home.

## MUDDLER

A muddler resembles a miniature rolling pin and is used to crush soft fruit and herbs in a glass. Always muddle ingredients in a glass that can handle the pressure, like a rocks glass.

## STRAINER

Officially known as a Hawthorn strainer, this tool fits over the top of the shaker. The small spring mechanism keeps ice and fruit chunks from falling into the glass.

# Glassware for Every Occasion

*You don't have to stock all these glasses at home, but depending on what kinds of drinks are your favorites, you might want to let a few of these share some shelf space with your wineglasses.*

### SHOT GLASS
Holds 1 ounce of liquid and can be used for measuring liquor for a cocktail or tossing back a quick swallow of alcohol

### ROCKS GLASS (also called an old fashioned or lowball)
A short, sturdy tumbler used for straight liquor over ice (such as scotch on the rocks) or cocktails that require just a splash of soda or juice, so as not to dilute the alcohol too much

### COLLINS GLASS (also called a tall glass)
Can be used for mixed drinks that require more dilution, such as a vodka tonic

### HIGHBALL
Generally taller than a Collins glass, this style was designed with towering fruity drinks in mind. Its height allows for lots of liquid and/or fruit, and it's a summer staple for serving refreshing, sweet cocktails.

### MARTINI GLASS (also called a cocktail glass)
This glass is best for short mixed cocktails, such as martinis, gimlets, and of course, cosmopolitans. Always hold it by the stem to avoid overheating the liquid in the glass. And sip provocatively, Cosmo girl!

# Metric Conversion Chart

*The recipes in this book are given in ounces (oz.), teaspoons (tsp.), tablespoons (Tbsp.), and cups. For readers who use metric measurements, here are the equivalents.*

| | | |
|---|---|---|
| ¼ oz. | = | .75 cl |
| ⅓ oz. | = | 1 cl |
| ½ oz. | = | 1.5 cl |
| ¾ oz. | = | 2.25 cl |
| 1 oz. | = | 3 cl |
| 1 cup | = | 24 cl |
| 1 tsp. | = | 5 ml |
| 1 Tbsp. | = | 15 ml |

# Liquors Worth a Shot

*Some of the sexy cocktails in our book call for rarer liquids that you may not recognize. Here's a quick guide. The exotic flavors they offer help create an unforgettable drink.*

### AGUA LUCA
Brazilian rum made from the juice of fresh sugarcane

### ALIZÉ BLEU
A blend of premium French vodka, cognac, passion fruit, cherry, ginger, and other natural exotic-fruit juices

### APEROL
Bright orange in color, this liqueur is an infusion of many herbs and roots and has a unique, bittersweet taste.

### BITTERS
An alcoholic beverage that is flavored with herbal essences and has a bitter or bittersweet flavor

### CASSIS
A bloodred, sweet, black-currant-flavored liqueur

### CHAMBORD
A sweet, black-raspberry-flavored liqueur

### CRÈME DE CACAO
A sweet alcoholic liqueur flavored primarily by the cocoa bean and the vanilla bean. It's also available in caramel-colored syrup, known as Dark Crème de Cacao, which has a chocolate flavor with hints of vanilla.

## CRÈME DE MENTHE

A very sweet mint-flavored liqueur. It comes in two versions: green and white (clear); there is no noticeable difference in flavor between the two.

## CRÈME DE NOYAUX

A red, almond-flavored liqueur made from fruit stones and sometimes made with peach or apricot pits

## CURAÇAO

A general term for orange-flavored liqueur made from the dried peel of bitter oranges found on the Caribbean island of Curaçao. Curaçao can be colored orange (known as Orange Curaçao or simply Curaçao), blue (Blue Curaçao), or green (Green Curaçao) or left clear (White Curaçao). All of them have the same flavor, with small variations in bitterness. Blue and Green Curaçao are often used to give color to mixed drinks.

## LILLET BLANC/LILLET ROUGE

A French aperitif made from a blend of wine, liqueurs, fruits, and herbs. Lillet Blanc is made from white wine; Lillet Rouge, from red.

## OUZO

This classic Greek drink is made from a combination of pressed grapes, herbs, and berries, including aniseed, licorice, mint, wintergreen, fennel, and hazelnut. Ouzo is usually served as an aperitif but is also used in some mixed drinks and cocktails.

## ST-GERMAIN

A French liqueur made from elderflowers

## TUACA

A vanilla citrus liqueur distilled from Mediterranean citrus fruits and Tuscan–style brandies

# Ask the Bartender

*Star mixologist Claire Smith answers the cocktail questions she gets asked most frequently.*

**Q: What are the most common mistakes that amateur bartenders make?**

**A:** The main one is not following measurements accurately—you want to be true to the recipe to make the best drinks. Also, amateurs often skimp on ice. It's important to serve a drink well chilled (except if it's meant to be hot, of course!). So unless the recipe tells you otherwise, use of plenty of rocks, whether you're shaking or stirring. Finally, make sure your garnishes don't overpower the drink—they should be complementary, not a distraction from what's in the glass.

**Q: Which kinds of liquor should I keep on hand in my liquor cabinet?**

**A:** The most obvious choice is vodka: It can be served chilled, in shots, and as the foundation of many cocktail recipes. But premium gin is another excellent base for simple, popular drinks that have a refreshing flavor. Keep a stash of both liquors so you'll be prepared for the most common requests.

**Q: If I don't have a certain alcohol, like tequila, can I use a substitution?**

**A:** Actually, it's best to use what you already have. If you have only rum, whip up some excellent rum cocktails instead of wishing you could make margaritas!

**Q: Are the glasses I use really that important?**

**A:** Well, they can definitely enhance the drinking experience. The thinner the lip of the glass, the more aeration the cocktail receives as it flows into your mouth. (Aeration lets you really savor the nuances of the drink.) But if you don't have every kind of cocktail glass, small wineglasses and champagne flutes are fantastic all-purpose cocktail glasses, and tumblers are great for a variety of drinks.

**Q: Which is more useful for me to have in my minibar: a blender or a shaker?**

**A:** Even though blenders are synonymous with frozen-drink fun, what you really need is a cocktail shaker. It chills the drink with ice, mixes the ingredients, and dilutes them with water. But a traditional shaker isn't essential—a jam jar will give you the same results. Wash it out thoroughly, secure the lid, and shake.

**Q: Is it okay to make a pitcher of pretty much anything? Or are some drinks better to make individually?**

**A:** Drinks that use fruit juice or soda are good to make in pitchers. Cocktails that use mainly high-proof ingredients are intended to be served very cold, so it's better to make those one at a time.

*Claire Smith, head of spirit creation and mixology for Belvedere Vodka, contributes cocktail recipes to Cosmo. Our faves include Berry Burst (p. 70) and The Pink Ginger (p. 82).*

# Index

· · · · · · · · · ·

# Photo Credits

## Cover

(Front cover and spine) Jesus Ayala/Studio D. Food and prop stylist: Nancy Sotomayor. Glasses: Williams-Sonoma.

(Back cover) (left to right, from top) Lara Robby/Studio D; Svend Lindbaek (2); Lara Robby/Studio D; Svend Lindbaek; Jack Miskell.

## Title Page

**PAGE 3:** Svend Lindbaek

## Table of Contents

**PAGE 5:** Lara Robby/Studio D

## Ready for Some Fun?

**PAGE 13:** Lara Robby/Studio D
**PAGE 14:** Svend Lindbaek
**PAGE 15:** Jesus Ayala/Studio D
**PAGE 16:** (From top) James Westman/Studio D; Philip Friedman/Studio D.
**PAGE 17:** Svend Lindbaek
**PAGE 18:** Chris Eckert/Studio D
**PAGE 20:** Jesus Ayala/Studio D
**PAGE 21:** (From top) Philip Friedman/Studio D; James Westman/Studio D.
**PAGE 22:** (From top) Jesus Ayala/Studio D. Food and prop stylist: Nancy Sotomayor. Glass: Crate & Barrel. Courtesy of Boston Public.
**PAGE 23:** Svend Lindbaek
**PAGE 24:** Jesus Ayala/Studio D. Food and prop stylist: Nancy Sotomayor. Glass: Crate & Barrel.
**PAGE 25:** Mark Lund

**PAGE 26:** Lara Robby/Studio D
**PAGE 28:** Chris Eckert/Studio D
**PAGE 29:** Chris Eckert/Studio D

## Get Your Flirt On!

**PAGE 33:** Svend Lindbaek
**PAGE 34:** Svend Lindbaek
**PAGE 35:** Chris Eckert/Studio D
**PAGE 36:** James Westman/Studio D
**PAGE 37:** Svend Lindbaek
**PAGE 38:** (From top) James Westman/Studio D; Jesus Ayala/Studio D.
**PAGE 39:** Svend Lindbaek
**PAGE 40:** Svend Lindbaek
**PAGE 42:** Svend Lindbaek
**PAGE 43:** Mark Lund
**PAGE 44:** Svend Lindbaek
**PAGE 45:** (From top) Jesus Ayala/Studio D; Lara Robby/Studio D.
**PAGE 46:** James Westman/Studio D
**PAGE 47:** Svend Lindbaek
**PAGE 48:** Svend Lindbaek
**PAGE 50:** Lara Robby/Studio D
**PAGE 51:** Jesus Ayala/Studio D

## Fearless & Fabulous

**PAGE 55:** Svend Lindbaek
**PAGE 56:** Svend Lindbaek
**PAGE 57:** James Westman/Studio D
**PAGE 58:** James Westman/Studio D
**PAGE 60:** Jesus Ayala/Studio D. Food and prop stylist: Nancy Sotomayor. Glass: Gracious Home.
**PAGE 61:** Svend Lindbaek
**PAGE 62:** Svend Lindbaek

Drink
Name:
_____

Ingredients:

_____    _____
_____    _____
_____    _____
_____    _____
_____    _____
_____    _____

Directions:

_____
_____
_____
_____
_____
_____

Notes:

_____
_____
_____

## Drink Name:

## Ingredients:

## Directions:

## Notes:

Drink
Name:
_____

Ingredients:

_____    _____
_____    _____
_____    _____
_____    _____
_____    _____
_____    _____

Directions:

_____
_____
_____
_____
_____
_____

Notes:

_____
_____
_____

Drink
Name:
_____

Ingredients:

_____   _____
_____   _____
_____   _____
_____   _____
_____   _____
_____   _____

Directions:

_____
_____
_____
_____
_____
_____

Notes:

_____
_____
_____

# COSMOPOLITAN

PROJECT DIRECTOR Susan Schulz
TEXT BY Bethany Heitman
BOOK DESIGN BY Peter Perron
COPYEDITED BY Katy Lindenmuth
EDITOR-IN-CHIEF Kate White
DESIGN DIRECTOR Ann P. Kwong

Library of Congress Cataloging-in-Publication Data

Cosmo's official cocktail book : the sexiest drinks for every occasion / the editors of *Cosmopolitan*.
   p. cm.
Includes index.
ISBN 978-1-58816-887-0
 1. Cocktails.  I. *Cosmopolitan* (New York, N.Y. : 1952) II. Title.

TX951.C7526 2010
 641.8'74—dc22

2010035537

10 9 8 7 6 5 4 3 2 1

Published by Hearst Books
A division of Sterling Publishing Co., Inc.
387 Park Avenue South, New York, NY 10016

*Cosmopolitan* is a registered trademark of Hearst Communications, Inc.

www.cosmopolitan.com

For information about custom editions, special sales, and premium and corporate purchases, please contact Sterling Special Sales Department at 800-805-5489 or specialsales@sterlingpublishing.com.

Distributed in Canada by Sterling Publishing
c/o Canadian Manda Group, 165 Dufferin Street
Toronto, Ontario, Canada M6K 3H6

Distributed in the United Kingdom by GMC Distribution Services
Castle Place, 166 High Street, Lewes, East Sussex, England BN7 1XU

Distributed in Australia by Capricorn Link (Australia) Pty. Ltd.
P.O. Box 704, Windsor, NSW 2756 Australia

Manufactured in China

Sterling ISBN 978-1-58816-887-0